From Paycheck to Prosperity

Escaping Paycheck-to-Paycheck and Building Generational Wealth, Even If You Think You Don't Earn Enough!

By Radhesh Reddy Gurrala

Self-published by **RayRan LLC**, Cary, NC, USA

ISBN: 9798285274506

Disclaimer: This book is intended to provide general information and education regarding personal finance, debt management, saving, investing, and wealth building. It is not intended as financial, legal, tax, or medical advice. The strategies discussed may not be suitable for all individuals, and past performance is not indicative of future results. You should consult with a qualified financial advisor, tax professional, and/or attorney to develop a personalized plan that is appropriate for your individual circumstances. The author and publisher disclaim any liability for any direct, indirect, or incidental damages resulting from the use of or reliance on the information contained herein.

Dedication

To my beloved family, whose unwavering love and support are the bedrock of my life and aspirations:

To my late mother, Manemma Gurrala, for bringing me into this world and standing by me until her last breath; her spirit continues to inspire me.

To my father and my guru, Rajumma Reddy Gurrala, for his foundational guidance.

To my brother, Venkat, for his lifelong camaraderie.

To my dear wife, Swetha, for her boundless patience and encouragement.

And to my incredible children, Rayan & Ranav, for whom I strive to build a legacy of abundance—not just of wealth, but of wisdom, resilience, and true freedom.

This book is also dedicated to every single person who believes they "don't earn enough" – may this blueprint empower you to redefine your financial reality.

Acknowledgements

My journey and the creation of this book would not have been possible without the immense contributions and unwavering belief of so many.

My deepest gratitude goes to my incredible teams at HGI Champs, Magicforce, and Cardinal Oaks Family for their dedication, hard work, and belief in this shared vision. Their tireless efforts behind the scenes are the engine of our collective success.

To my cherished mentors and friends, thank you for your invaluable guidance, support, and friendship throughout this writing process. Your insights and encouragement were truly indispensable.

And finally, to the countless individuals who have bravely shared their financial struggles and triumphs with me over the years – your stories are the authentic heartbeat of this book and the profound inspiration behind every page. Thank you for your trust and your courage; this work is dedicated to your transformation.

Table of Contents

Introduction: The Urgent Call to Financial Freedom

Does this sound familiar?

You work hard. You clock in, you put in the hours, you bring home a paycheck. Yet, by the time the next payday rolls around, your bank account feels strangely empty. You might even have dipped into savings – or worse, relied on credit cards – just to make it through. You glance at your bills, sigh, and think, "I just don't earn enough to get ahead. My money disappears before I even have a chance to breathe."

This isn't just a feeling; it's a trap. It's the **paycheck-to-paycheck cycle**, a pervasive reality for millions, regardless of their income level. It's a cycle fueled by debt, rising costs, and, most powerfully, a deeply ingrained belief that there simply isn't enough money to go around.

But what if I told you that this cycle is not your destiny? What if I showed you a clear, actionable path to break free, not just to survive, but to **thrive**? This isn't about getting rich quick, winning the lottery, or inheriting a fortune. This is about transforming your relationship with money, unlocking hidden potential in your current income, and systematically building a financial future that extends far beyond your own lifetime – **generational wealth.**

This book is a direct response to that nagging thought, "I don't earn enough." I know that thought because I've heard it countless times, and in different seasons of life, I've felt it too. It's a paralyzing belief that stops people from taking action. But here's the profound truth: **it's rarely about how much you earn, and almost always about how you manage what you do earn.**

This isn't a book filled with complex financial jargon or impossible demands. It's a step-by-step blueprint designed for real people living real lives. We will strip away the overwhelm and provide practical, compassionate guidance to help you:

- **Unmask your money mindset:** Identify the limiting beliefs that hold you back.
- **Master your money:** Get crystal clear on where your money goes and how to direct it with intention.
- **Demolish debt:** Create a powerful plan to eliminate financial shackles that keep you stuck.
- **Build a financial fortress:** Establish emergency savings and essential insurance to protect your progress.
- **Unlock the power of your existing income:** Turn saving and investing into

achievable habits, proving you *do* earn enough to grow your wealth.

- **Expand your earning potential:** Discover strategies to bring in more income, accelerating your journey.
- **Protect your legacy:** Understand how to ensure your hard-earned wealth benefits future generations.

This is more than just a finance book; it's a guide to reclaiming your power, building confidence, and creating a future of true abundance. You are capable of so much more than just surviving paycheck to paycheck. You are capable of building lasting wealth. Let's begin.

Part 1: The Foundation - Escaping the Paycheck-to-Paycheck Cycle

Chapter 1: Unmasking Your Money Mindset & Habits

Imagine two people earning the exact same income. One consistently struggles, living paycheck-to-paycheck, accumulating debt. The other builds savings, invests, and feels a growing sense of financial peace. What's the difference? It's rarely about their income; it's almost always about their **money mindset** and deeply ingrained habits.

You've picked up this book because you feel that nagging sensation: "I don't earn enough." That thought, while common, is a powerful indicator that your money mindset needs attention. Before we talk about budgets, debt, or investments, we must first look inward. Because if your beliefs about money are rooted in scarcity, fear, or a sense of powerlessness, even the best strategies will crumble.

What is a Money Mindset?

Your money mindset is the sum total of your beliefs, attitudes, and feelings about money. It's shaped by your upbringing, cultural background, personal experiences, and even the media you consume. These beliefs, often unconscious, drive your financial behaviors.

Consider these common money mindsets:

- **Scarcity Mindset:** "There's never enough money." "Money is hard to come by." "If I spend money, I'll never get it back." This often leads to hoarding or, paradoxically, reckless spending out of fear it will disappear.
- **Abundance Mindset:** "There is always enough." "Money flows easily." "I can create wealth." This fosters a sense of possibility and encourages strategic management.
- **Victim Mindset:** "Money problems always happen to me." "It's not my fault; the economy/my boss/my circumstances are to blame." This prevents taking responsibility and action.
- **"Money is Evil" Mindset:** "Rich people are greedy." "Money corrupts." This can lead to self-sabotage, preventing you from accumulating wealth.
- **"Money is Freedom" Mindset:** "Money is a tool for choice and opportunity." This sees money as a means to achieve life goals.

Which of these resonates most strongly with you right now? Understanding your starting point is crucial.

Unearthing Your Money Story

Your money mindset isn't random; it's a story you've been told, or have told yourself.

Where did it come from?

- **Childhood Experiences:** What did your parents or guardians say about money? Were they stressed about it? Did they hide money troubles? Were they generous or frugal? Did they teach you about saving?
- **Significant Life Events:** A period of poverty, a sudden inheritance, a job loss, a financial crisis – these events can deeply imprint beliefs about money.
- **Cultural & Societal Messages:** What messages about wealth, poverty, work, and spending do you absorb from your community, media, or peers?

The goal isn't to blame your past, but to understand its influence. Once you make the unconscious conscious, you gain the power to change it.

Your Current Money Habits: The Reflection of Your Mindset

Your actions speak louder than your unconscious thoughts. What do your current money habits reveal?

- **Spending Habits:** Do you spend compulsively? Are you a "splurger" or a "saver"? Do you know where your money goes?
- **Saving Habits:** Do you save consistently? Is it an automatic priority, or an afterthought?
- **Debt Habits:** Do you use credit cards for everyday expenses? Do you carry a balance? Do you avoid looking at your debt statements?
- **Earnings Habits:** Do you believe you're worth more? Do you negotiate your salary? Do you explore ways to increase your income?

This isn't about judgment; it's about honest assessment. Your habits are simply learned behaviors that can be unlearned and replaced with new ones.

The First Step to Transformation: Awareness & Micro-Shifts

You might feel overwhelmed, thinking, "I have to change *everything*." No, you don't. Start with small, deliberate steps. These micro-shifts begin to rewire your brain and prove to yourself that change is possible.

1. **Acknowledge the Belief:** When you hear yourself think, "I don't earn enough," pause. Acknowledge the thought without judgment. Then, gently challenge it: "Is that truly 100% accurate, or am I operating from a belief?"
2. **Practice Gratitude for What You Have:** Even if it feels small, focusing on financial gratitude shifts you from scarcity to abundance. Be grateful for your income, your

home, your food, your ability to pay any bill.

3. **Start a "Money Wins" Jar (Mental or Physical):** Every time you make a positive financial choice—saving $5, paying a bill on time, resisting an impulse purchase—acknowledge it. These small wins build momentum and prove your capability.

4. **Conscious Spending Journal:** For just one week, write down *every single dollar* you spend and how it makes you *feel.* Was it regret? Joy? Necessity? Boredom? This illuminates emotional spending triggers.

This initial stage of unmasking your mindset and habits is perhaps the most crucial. Without this foundational work, any financial strategy will feel like a struggle against an invisible current. By facing your beliefs and understanding your behaviors, you're already taking the first powerful step towards proving to yourself that you *do* earn enough to build financial freedom.

Your Next Steps: Unmask Your Money Story

1. **Money Script Self-Assessment:** Take a few minutes to write down 3-5 of your earliest memories or messages about money. What did you hear or observe? How did they make you feel?

2. **Emotional Spending Journal:** For the next 3 days, track every single dollar you spend. Next to each expense, jot down how you felt before, during, and after the purchase. (e.g., "Coffee - tired, momentary satisfaction, regret").

3. **"Find Your First Five" Challenge:** Find $5 that you can consciously save or put towards a debt today. It might be by skipping a small purchase, finding coins, or selling something tiny. Just find it and set it aside deliberately. This builds immediate momentum.

Chapter 2: Know Your Numbers: The Budgeting Breakthrough

The idea of budgeting often evokes dread. For many, it feels like a financial straitjacket, restricting fun, and forcing you to confront the uncomfortable truth that you "don't earn enough" to cover everything. You might have tried budgeting before and given up, or perhaps avoided it entirely, believing it's too complicated or too restrictive.

But here's the truth: **budgeting isn't about deprivation; it's about liberation.** It's not about cutting out joy; it's about intentionally directing your money towards what truly matters to you. It's the essential tool that transforms that vague, anxious feeling of "not enough" into a crystal-clear understanding of exactly where your money goes, giving you the power to tell every dollar where to go.

This chapter will simplify budgeting, showing you how to get clear on your numbers without judgment, and how to build a budget that actually works for *your* life.

The Purpose of a Budget: Your Financial Roadmap

Think of your budget as a personalized financial roadmap. It's not a punishment; it's a plan.

- **Awareness:** It reveals exactly where your money is going. Often, we underestimate how much we spend on small, discretionary items.
- **Control:** It gives you the power to decide where your money goes, rather than wondering where it went.
- **Goal Achievement:** It's how you allocate funds for your dreams—whether it's getting out of debt, building an emergency fund, saving for a down payment, or investing.
- **Reduced Stress:** When you know your numbers, you replace anxiety with clarity and intention. This directly combats the "not enough" belief by showing you the truth of your financial situation.

Calculate Your Net Income: The Starting Point

Before you can budget, you need to know exactly how much money you have to work with. This is your **net income**, often called your "take-home pay."

- **Gross Income:** Your total earnings before any taxes or deductions are taken out.
- **Net Income:** The amount that actually lands in your bank account after all deductions (federal and state taxes, Social Security, Medicare, retirement contributions, health insurance premiums) have been withheld.

Actionable Step: Find Your Net Income:

Gather your pay stubs for the last month or two. Your net income is the amount you actually receive. If you're paid bi-weekly, multiply that number by 2 to get your monthly net income. If you have multiple income sources (like a side hustle), add all net incomes together.

My Monthly Net Income: $_____

The 30-Day Spending Track: Your Financial Reality Check

Before you make any cuts, you need to see your actual spending habits. This is not about judgment, just observation.

- **The Method:** For the next 30 days, track *every single dollar* you spend.
  - **Old School:** Carry a small notebook and pen, jotting down every expense immediately.
  - **Tech Savvy:** Use a budgeting app (Mint, YNAB, EveryDollar) or a spreadsheet on your phone. Many apps can link directly to your bank accounts for easy tracking.
- **Categorize:** Group your spending. Common categories include: Housing (rent/mortgage), Utilities, Groceries, Transportation (gas, public transport), Debt Payments, Dining Out, Entertainment, Personal Care, Shopping, Subscriptions, Miscellaneous.
- **Be Brutally Honest:** Don't omit anything, no matter how small or seemingly insignificant. That daily coffee or infrequent impulse buy adds up!

Building Your Budget: Giving Every Dollar a Job

Once you have your net income and your 30-day spending track, you have the data to create your plan. Here are popular budgeting methods:

1. **The Zero-Based Budget (Recommended for Debt Demolition):**
   - **Concept:** Every dollar of your net income is assigned a "job" until your income minus your expenses (and savings/debt payments) equals zero. This ensures intentionality.
   - **How:** List your income. Then list all your expenses and savings goals. Assign every dollar. If you have money left over, assign it to debt or savings. If you're in the negative, you know you need to adjust.

- Why it works: It eliminates financial ambiguity. There's no "leftover" money to wonder about. It actively combats the "not enough" feeling by forcing you to allocate *all* your income.

2. **The 50/30/20 Rule:**
   - **Concept:** A simpler guideline: 50% of your net income for Needs, 30% for Wants, 20% for Savings & Debt Repayment.
   - **Needs (50%):** Housing, utilities, groceries, transportation, minimum debt payments, essential insurance.
   - **Wants (30%):** Dining out, entertainment, shopping, vacations, subscriptions.
   - **Savings & Debt Repayment (20%):** Emergency fund, extra debt payments, investments, retirement.
   - **Why it works:** It's a quick way to assess if your spending is roughly in line. If your "Needs" are eating up more than 50%, you know where to focus.

3. **The Envelope System (Cash-Based):**
   - **Concept:** For variable expenses (like groceries, dining out, entertainment), you withdraw cash and place it into physical envelopes. When the money in the envelope is gone, you stop spending in that category until the next budget period.
   - **Why it works:** Provides a strong visual and tactile constraint, excellent for curbing overspending.

Actionable Step: Choose Your Method & Categorize

Pick one method and start categorizing your spending from the 30-day track into "Needs" vs. "Wants."

Making Your Budget Work: Flexibility & Review

Your first budget won't be perfect. And that's okay!

- **Be Flexible:** Life happens. You'll overspend in one category, underspend in another. Adjust your budget as needed. The goal is progress, not perfection.
- **Review Regularly:** At least once a month, review your spending against your budget. Did you stick to it? Where did you overspend? Where did you save? What needs adjusting for next month?
- **Communicate (If in a partnership):** If you share finances, budgeting must be a joint effort. Discuss openly, set goals together, and respect each other's contributions.

By consistently knowing your numbers and giving every dollar a job, you transform your financial landscape. You replace confusion with clarity, anxiety with control. You begin to see that your income, while perhaps not limitless, is indeed enough to manage your expenses, pay down debt, and build for the future. The feeling of "not enough" begins to fade, replaced by a powerful sense of intention and capability.

Your Next Steps: Master Your Money Map

1. **Net Income Calculation:** Confirm your exact monthly net (take-home) income.
2. **30-Day Spending Track:** Start tracking every single dollar you spend for the next 30 days. Don't change your habits yet; just observe.
3. **Choose a Budgeting Method:** Based on your personality and goals, decide whether the Zero-Based Budget, 50/30/20 Rule, or Envelope System (or a combination) feels right for you.
4. **Draft Your First Budget:** At the end of your 30-day track, sit down and draft your first budget based on your chosen method and actual spending. Give every dollar a job!

Chapter 3: The Debt Demolition Plan

If you're caught in the paycheck-to-paycheck cycle, chances are, debt is a heavy anchor dragging you down. Credit card balances, car loans, student loans, personal loans – these aren't just numbers on a statement. They represent past choices, often made out of necessity or lack of financial knowledge, that now siphon away your present income and fuel the belief that you "don't earn enough."

The constant pressure of minimum payments, the crushing interest rates, and the feeling that you're always just treading water are emotionally and financially exhausting. It makes achieving any other financial goal feel impossible.

This chapter isn't about shaming; it's about empowering. We're going to expose the true cost of debt and then give you two powerful, actionable strategies to systematically demolish it. Freeing yourself from debt is not just about numbers; it's about reclaiming your income, your peace of mind, and your future.

The True Cost of Debt: More Than Just Payments

It's easy to focus only on the minimum payment, but debt costs you far more than that.

- **Interest:** This is the silent killer. A credit card with a 20% APR (Annual Percentage Rate) means that for every $100 you carry, you're paying $20 *per year* just for the privilege of borrowing. Over time, you can pay back multiples of what you originally spent.
- **Lost Opportunity:** Every dollar you send to a creditor in interest is a dollar you *cannot* save for your emergency fund, invest for retirement, or put towards a down payment. It's money you work for that never comes back to you.
- **Stress & Anxiety:** Debt is a heavy mental burden. It impacts your sleep, relationships, and overall well-being.
- **Erosion of Income:** When a significant portion of your paycheck is allocated to minimum payments, it absolutely reinforces the feeling that you "don't earn enough." Getting rid of debt is like giving yourself an immediate pay raise.

Your Debt Inventory: Facing the Monster

You cannot defeat what you don't fully understand. The first step is to gather all your debt information in one place. This can be intimidating, but it's crucial. Take a deep breath.

Actionable Step: Debt Inventory Worksheet

Gather all your statements (credit cards, personal loans, car loans, student loans). For each debt, write down:

- **Creditor:** (e.g., Visa Card, Student Loan Co.)
- **Current Balance:**
- **Interest Rate (APR):**
- **Minimum Monthly Payment:**

Creditor	Balance	Interest Rate (APR)	Min. Monthly Payment

Order your debts from smallest balance to largest (for Debt Snowball) OR from highest interest rate to lowest (for Debt Avalanche).

Choosing Your Demolition Method: Snowball vs. Avalanche

Both methods are powerful. Choose the one that best fits your personality and motivation.

1. **The Debt Snowball (Recommended for Motivation & Momentum):**
   - **How it works:** List your debts from the *smallest balance to the largest*, regardless of interest rate. Pay the minimum payment on all debts except the smallest one. Throw every extra dollar you can find at that smallest debt until it's gone. Once it's paid off, you take the money you were paying on that debt (its minimum payment + any extra) and apply it to the *next* smallest debt. You roll the payment like a snowball, building momentum.
   - **Why it works:** Creates quick wins and psychological victories. Seeing debts disappear, even small ones, builds confidence and motivation, making it easier

to stick with the plan long-term. This is powerful for combating the "not enough" mindset, as you see tangible results.

- ○ *Best for:* Those who need quick wins to stay motivated.

2. **The Debt Avalanche (Recommended for Mathematical Efficiency):**
   - ○ **How it works:** List your debts from the *highest interest rate to the lowest,* regardless of balance. Pay the minimum payment on all debts except the one with the highest interest rate. Throw every extra dollar you can find at that highest-interest debt until it's gone. Once it's paid off, you take the money you were paying on that debt and apply it to the *next* highest-interest debt.
   - ○ **Why it works:** Saves you the most money in interest over the long run.
   - ○ *Best for:* Those who are highly motivated by numbers and efficiency.

Fueling Your Demolition: Finding Extra Money

Now, the crucial question: "Where will I find the extra money to throw at my debt, especially if I already feel I don't earn enough?" This is where your efforts from Chapter 2 become powerful.

- **"Debt Fuel" from Your Budget:** Go back to your budget. Are there any "wants" that you can temporarily cut or reduce drastically? Dining out, entertainment, subscriptions, impulse shopping – even small sacrifices add up. Every dollar you free up goes directly to your debt.
- **Temporary Income Boosts:**
  - ○ **Side Hustles:** Can you pick up extra shifts, deliver groceries, or offer a skill for a few extra hours a week? Every extra dollar from a side hustle (Chapter 9 discusses this more) goes straight to debt.
  - ○ **Sell Unused Items:** Declutter your home and sell clothes, electronics, furniture, or anything you no longer need. This isn't just about money; it's about simplifying your life.
  - ○ **Bonuses or Tax Refunds:** Designate 100% of any windfalls directly to debt until it's gone.
- **Negotiate Interest Rates:** Call your credit card companies and ask for a lower interest rate, especially if you have a good payment history. Even a few percentage points can save you money.

Your Debt-Free Life Awaits

Demolishing debt is hard work, but it's some of the most rewarding work you'll ever do. Every payment chips away at the chains that bind you to the paycheck-to-paycheck cycle. As each debt falls, you'll not only save on interest but experience an incredible surge of financial freedom. The money you were sending to creditors becomes **your** money, ready to be directed towards building your financial fortress and future wealth. This is how you prove to yourself, unequivocally, that you *do* earn enough to be debt-free.

Your Next Steps: Ignite Your Demolition

1. **Complete Your Debt Inventory:** Don't skip this step. Gather all your debt information and organize it.
2. **Choose Your Demolition Method:** Decide whether the Debt Snowball or Debt Avalanche is right for you.
3. **"Find Your Debt Fuel" Challenge:** Brainstorm 3-5 specific ways you will find extra money *this month* to throw at your debt (e.g., "cut daily coffee = $X," "sell old electronics = $Y," "work Z extra hours at side job = $Z").
4. **Set Your First Debt-Free Date:** Use an online debt payoff calculator (search "debt snowball calculator" or "debt avalanche calculator") to see how quickly you can become debt-free by applying extra payments. This visualization is incredibly motivating!

Chapter 4: Building Your Financial Fortress: Emergency Funds & Insurance

You've faced your money mindset, you've exposed where every dollar goes, and you're now actively demolishing debt. You're building incredible momentum! But here's a hard truth: life has a way of throwing curveballs. The car breaks down, an unexpected medical bill arrives, the water heater decides to retire, or, most daunting of all, a job loss occurs.

For someone caught in the paycheck-to-paycheck cycle, these aren't just inconveniences; they're catastrophic events. They're the moments that often force you to grab a credit card, wipe out any progress you've made, and send you spiraling right back into the cycle of struggle. It's in these moments that the familiar, agonizing thought screams loudest: "I just don't have enough money to handle this."

Many people mistakenly believe an **emergency fund** is a luxury, something only for those who "have enough" to begin with. But I'm here to tell you that it's the most fundamental step to *creating* enough. Without it, every unexpected expense will continue to prove that you *don't* have enough, forcing you back to square one, or worse, deeper into debt. An emergency fund isn't a want; it's a non-negotiable shield against life's inevitable storms.

What is an Emergency Fund and Why It's Non-Negotiable

Simply put, an **emergency fund** is a separate savings account specifically designed to cover unexpected, unavoidable financial emergencies. This isn't for a vacation, a new gadget, or holiday gifts. This money is solely for:

- **Job loss:** Covering essential expenses until you find new employment.
- **Medical emergencies:** Unforeseen doctor visits, prescriptions, or hospital bills.
- **Car repairs:** That blown tire or engine trouble that pops up without warning.
- **Home repairs:** A leaky roof, a broken appliance, or a burst pipe.

Having this fund provides immense **peace of mind.** It allows you to absorb financial shocks without having to go back into debt, borrow from friends, or dip into funds meant for your long-term goals. It's the ultimate debt prevention tool, directly addressing the feeling that you "don't have enough" by creating a buffer for when life gets tough.

How Much to Save: Building Layers of Protection

Building your emergency fund doesn't happen overnight, and that's okay. We'll approach it in layers, building momentum just like you did with your debt demolition:

1. **Layer 1: The Starter Fund ($1,000 - $2,000)**
   - **Your immediate goal.** This initial amount is enough to cover many common minor emergencies. It's your first significant barrier against falling back into credit card debt for unexpected expenses. Achieving this early win will dramatically boost your confidence.

2. **Layer 2: 3-6 Months of Essential Expenses**
   - **The ultimate goal.** Once your starter fund is solid, you'll work towards accumulating enough to cover 3 to 6 months of your **essential living expenses.** Think about your absolute "needs" from Chapter 2's budget: housing, utilities, basic groceries, transportation, minimum debt payments, and essential insurance.
   - **Why 3-6 months?** This provides a crucial safety net for bigger events like a job loss, allowing you time to recover without panicking or making rash financial decisions. If your job security is lower, or you have dependents, aim for the higher end of this range.

Actionable Step: Calculate Your Emergency Fund Targets

Go back to your budget from Chapter 2 and list your true essential monthly expenses. Then calculate:

- **Your Starter Fund Target:** ($1,000 or $2,000, whichever feels more achievable first): $_____
- **Your 3-Month Essential Expenses Target:** (Your monthly essential expenses x 3): $_____
- **Your 6-Month Essential Expenses Target:** (Your monthly essential expenses x 6): $_____

Where to Keep Your Emergency Fund

Your emergency fund needs to be:

- **Accessible:** You should be able to get to it quickly if a true emergency arises.
- **Safe:** It should be in an FDIC-insured account, meaning your money is protected by the government up to $250,000.
- **Separate:** Don't keep it in your checking account, where it's easily confused with spending money.
- **Growing (Ideally):** Look for a **high-yield savings account (HYSA)**. These are offered by online banks and pay significantly higher interest rates than traditional brick-and-mortar banks, helping your money grow faster while remaining liquid. Avoid investing your emergency fund in the stock market, as its value can fluctuate, and you can't risk losing it when you need it most.

Strategies for Building Your Emergency Fund

Remember all that money you've started to free up from debt demolition (Chapter 3) and those "money leaks" you plugged with your budgeting efforts (Chapter 2)? This is where that money goes first, before anything else!

- **Automate Your Savings:** This is the most powerful strategy. Set up an automatic transfer from your checking account to your HYSA every payday, even if it's just $25 or $50 to start. "Out of sight, out of mind" works wonders here.
- **Direct Windfalls:** Any unexpected money—a bonus, a tax refund, a small inheritance, a birthday gift—goes straight into your emergency fund until it's fully funded. Resist the urge to splurge.
- **Designate Side Hustle Income:** If you've started a side hustle, consider directing 100% of that income to your emergency fund until it meets your target.
- **Continue Temporary Cuts:** Maintain some of the "debt fuel" mentality from Chapter 3 for a short period. This focused intensity can get your starter fund built quickly.

The Shield of Insurance: Protecting What You've Built

While your emergency fund handles smaller, unpredictable events, **insurance** is your safety net against catastrophic financial loss. It's easy to view insurance as just another bill, another expense that reinforces the feeling of "not enough." But properly structured insurance is a critical component of your financial fortress; it protects your wealth, your health, and your future.

You don't need every type of insurance, but certain policies are non-negotiable. Focus on insuring against events that could financially devastate you.

Essential Types of Insurance You Need:

1. **Health Insurance:** Absolutely critical. A single medical emergency without insurance can wipe out years of savings and plunge you into crushing debt. Whether through your employer, a spouse's plan, or the Affordable Care Act (ACA) marketplace, make sure you're covered.

2. **Auto Insurance:** If you drive, it's legally required in most places. It protects you financially in case of an accident, covering damages to your vehicle, other vehicles, and medical expenses for injuries.

3. **Homeowner's or Renter's Insurance:** If you own, homeowner's insurance protects your house and belongings from damage or theft. If you rent, **renter's insurance** is an affordable must-have. It protects your personal belongings from theft, fire, or other covered perils, and also provides liability coverage if someone gets hurt in your rented space. Many people renting skip this, but replacing all your belongings after a fire is a massive financial blow.

4. **Life Insurance (If you have dependents):** If anyone relies on your income (children, spouse, elderly parents), life insurance is non-negotiable. It provides a financial safety net for them if you pass away prematurely. For most people, **term life insurance** is the best choice—it's affordable, straightforward, and covers you for a specific period (e.g., 20 or 30 years) when your dependents are most vulnerable. Avoid complex whole life or universal life policies unless advised by a trusted, fee-only financial planner for specific advanced situations.

5. **Long-Term Disability Insurance:** This is often overlooked but vital. What if you couldn't work for months or years due to illness or injury? Disability insurance replaces a portion of your income, protecting your ability to pay your bills and continue your financial journey. If your employer offers it, enroll. If not, explore individual policies.

Key Principles for Insurance:

- **Insure against catastrophe, not inconvenience.** Don't over-insure things you can easily replace.
- **Shop around.** Get quotes from multiple providers annually for auto and home/renter's insurance.
- **Understand your policy.** Know your deductibles and coverage limits.

The Ultimate Financial Peace

Building a fully funded emergency fund and securing proper insurance are acts of profound financial self-care. This is where the belief of "not enough money" truly starts to fade. You're not just earning; you're building a robust buffer, a protection that allows you to absorb financial shocks without falling back into the cycle of struggle. This foundation allows you to take risks, pursue opportunities, and genuinely start thinking about wealth creation, knowing you have a shield against life's inevitable challenges. It's the peace of mind that allows you to breathe, knowing you're truly building prosperity.

Your Next Steps: Fortify Your Finances

1. **Calculate Your Emergency Fund Targets:** Go back and fill in those dollar amounts for your Starter Fund and 3-6 month targets.
2. **Emergency Fund Action Plan:** List 3-5 specific, realistic actions you will take *this month* to start funding your emergency fund. (e.g., "Automate $50 transfer each payday," "Sell X old item for $Y," "Direct side hustle income to fund.")
3. **Conduct an Insurance Audit:**
   - Do you have health, auto, homeowner's/renter's insurance?
   - If you have dependents, do you have life insurance?
   - Do you have disability insurance through work or privately?
   - Are there any critical gaps? Make a note to research any missing essential policies or to shop for better rates.
4. **Automate It!** Set up that automatic transfer to your new, separate high-yield savings account for your emergency fund. This is the single most important step.

Chapter 5: The Power of Saving: Beyond the Emergency Fund

You've come so far. You've bravely confronted your money mindset, mapped out your income and expenses, started demolishing debt, and are now building your financial fortress with an emergency fund. You are no longer merely reacting to your financial situation; you are actively taking control. This is a monumental shift.

For many, once the emergency fund is established (or even just started), the urge to relax or spend what feels like "extra" money can be strong. You might even hear that familiar whisper: "I've done enough. I still don't earn *that* much, so this is probably as good as it gets for saving."

But this chapter marks a crucial transition. We're moving from financial defense to **offense**. Saving is no longer just about protecting against disaster; it's about actively building the future you envision. It's about consciously directing your income towards your dreams, proving to yourself, dollar by dollar, that your income *is* sufficient for more than just bills.

Why Saving is Critical for Wealth Building (Beyond Emergencies)

Think of saving as the fuel in your financial engine. Your emergency fund is the protective casing, but goal-oriented savings are what actually drive you forward. This dedicated saving:

- **Accumulates Capital:** You need a lump sum for larger purchases or investment opportunities. Saving provides that capital.
- **Provides Flexibility & Options:** A robust savings habit means you have choices. Want to pursue a new skill? Change careers? Take a sabbatical? Savings can make it possible.
- **Strengthens Financial Muscles:** The discipline of consistent saving directly prepares you for the even greater discipline of consistent investing. It proves you can commit to long-term financial goals.
- **Boosts Confidence:** Every dollar saved for a specific goal is a tangible win, reinforcing that you *can* manage your money effectively, directly combating the "I don't earn enough" narrative.

Short-Term, Mid-Term, Long-Term: Giving Your Money a Mission

Not all savings are created equal. Each dollar you save needs a mission, a purpose. This helps you stay motivated and prevents you from dipping into funds intended for different goals.

- **Short-Term Goals (0-2 years):** These are your immediate desires. Think of them as exciting milestones that keep you engaged.
  - *Examples:* A dream vacation, new furniture, upgrading an essential appliance, holiday spending fund (so you don't use credit cards in December!), a down payment for a slightly better car, or even a fund for a special splurge that feels genuinely meaningful.

- **Mid-Term Goals (3-5 years):** These require a bit more planning and dedication, but offer significant payoff.
  - *Examples:* A significant down payment on a home, funding for further education or professional certification, a major car purchase paid in cash, or building a fund to bridge income during a career change or to start a small business.

- **Long-Term Goals (5+ years):** While we'll dive deeper into retirement in a later chapter, consider other long-term aspirations here.
  - *Examples:* A child's education fund, a fund for a significant life event (wedding, sabbatical), or accumulating a larger sum for a future, more complex investment.

Actionable Step: Define Your Savings Missions

Now, it's your turn. What are 1-3 short-term goals and 1-2 mid-term goals that truly excite you? Be specific with what you want to save for, how much it will cost, and by when you'd like to achieve it.

Goal Type	Specific Goal (e.g., Summer vacation to Florida)	Estimated Cost	Target Date (Month/Year)
Short-Term			
Short-Term			
Mid-Term			
Mid-Term			

The Power of Automation & Dedicated Accounts

The golden rule of successful saving is **automation**. If you wait until the end of the month to see what's left over to save, chances are, there won't be anything. You need to set up your savings to happen *before* you even see the money.

- **Automate, Automate, Automate:** Just like you would pay a bill, set up automatic transfers from your checking account to your dedicated savings accounts (still using high-yield savings accounts for liquidity and interest, as discussed in Chapter 4). Set these transfers to happen on payday. Even if it's just $25 or $50 to start for each goal, this consistency is powerful.

- **Separate Accounts:** This might seem like overkill, but having clearly labeled savings accounts for each goal (e.g., "Vacation Fund," "Down Payment Fund," "Car Repair Fund") provides psychological clarity and prevents you from "borrowing" from one goal to fund another. Your bank might allow you to nickname different savings accounts, or you can use different online HYSA providers for each.

By automating, you bypass the emotional debate of "Can I afford to save?" The money is simply moved, proving to yourself that you *can* afford it, and that your income *is* enough.

Finding the Money for Your Goals

"Okay," you might be thinking, "this sounds great, but *where* exactly is this extra money coming from, especially if I still feel like I don't earn enough?" This is where your meticulous work in Chapter 2 (budgeting) and Chapter 3 (debt demolition) truly shines:

- **Reallocate from Debt Payments:** As you pay off debts, especially those higher-interest ones, the money you were sending to creditors is now **freed up**. Instead of letting it disappear into general spending, immediately reallocate it to your savings goals. This is often the single biggest source of "new" money for saving.
- **Identify More Money Leaks:** Continue to review your variable expenses. Are there any more non-essential "wants" that you can temporarily reduce or cut to accelerate your savings goals? Every dollar you redirect from unconscious spending to intentional saving is a win.
- **Turbocharge with Income Boosts:** Remember the side hustles and income-boosting strategies we touched on in Chapter 3? Dedicate a portion (or even all!) of any extra income you earn—bonuses, tax refunds, a raise, a side gig—directly to your savings goals. This can dramatically shorten the time it takes to reach your targets.

The Magic of Compound Interest (Even in Savings)

You might associate compound interest primarily with investing, but its power begins even with basic savings. Compound interest means your money earns interest, and then *that interest* also starts earning interest. It's money making money, and it's the reason why starting early, even with small amounts, is so impactful.

Imagine saving just $50 consistently each month into a high-yield savings account earning a modest 4% interest (far more than most checking accounts). Over five years, you would have saved $3,000 in principal. But thanks to compound interest, your balance would be closer to $3,200. That extra $200 is literally money you earned by simply saving!

This principle is fundamental to wealth creation. Every dollar you intentionally save today isn't just a static dollar; it's a seed you're planting that will grow over time, continually reinforcing that you *do* have the capacity to build wealth.

Overcoming Saving Obstacles

You might encounter some mental roadblocks:

- **"It's too small to matter"**: Counter this by remembering the power of consistency and compound interest. A tiny drip fills a bucket over time.
- **"I'll save tomorrow"**: This is the voice of procrastination, and it's the thief of your future. Start *now*, even with a small amount.
- **"Emergencies keep draining my savings"**: This highlights why your fully funded emergency fund (Chapter 4) is so crucial. It acts as the guardian, protecting your goal-oriented savings from being raided by unexpected events.

By consciously directing your income towards specific, exciting goals, you're not just stashing cash; you're building a clear path to the life you want. You are proving, once and for all, that you *do* earn enough to save, to achieve your aspirations, and to lay the groundwork for true financial freedom. The next step? Making that money work even harder by investing it.

Your Next Steps: Fuel Your Future

1. **Finalize Your Savings Goals:** Complete the table above for your 1-3 short-term and 1-2 mid-term goals, with realistic amounts and target dates.
2. **Create Your Savings Allocation Plan:** Look at your budget (Chapter 2) and any freed-up debt payments (Chapter 3). How much can you realistically automate towards *each* of your new savings goals every payday? Write down the specific dollar amount for each goal.
3. **Automate It (Again!):** Set up auto-transfers for your new savings goals to your new, separate high-yield savings account. This is the single most important step.
4. **(Optional) Visualize Compound Interest:** Use a simple online compound interest calculator to visualize how your consistent savings, even small amounts, can grow over time. This can be a powerful motivator.

Part 2: The Ascent - Mastering Your Money for Growth

Chapter 6: Understanding Investing: Your Wealth-Building Engine

You've built a solid financial foundation. Your mindset is shifting, your budget is clear, debt is being demolished, and your emergency fund stands as a strong fortress. Now, it's time for your money to truly start working for you, tirelessly, 24/7. It's time to talk about **investing.**

For many, the word "investing" conjures images of complex stock tickers, confusing jargon, and high-stakes gambles on Wall Street, reserved only for millionaires or financial gurus. You might have thought, "I don't earn enough to invest," or "It's too risky for someone like me."

This is one of the most persistent and damaging myths for someone trying to escape the paycheck-to-paycheck cycle. The truth is, **investing is not a privilege of the wealthy; it is how wealth is built.** It's the engine that will power your journey from financial stability to true generational prosperity. Without investing, your money loses purchasing power over time, swallowed by inflation. With it, your money grows, compounds, and creates a future you might currently only dream of.

This chapter will demystify investing, breaking down the basics into understandable concepts and showing you how you can start, regardless of your current income.

Why Investing is Essential: The Enemy of Inflation

Imagine your $100 today. In 20 years, will it buy the same amount of groceries or cover the same expenses? Probably not. This is due to **inflation**, the gradual increase in prices over time. If your money just sits in a regular savings account, it's actually losing value year after year.

Investing is how you fight back against inflation. It's how you make your money grow faster than the rate of rising prices, preserving and increasing your purchasing power over the long term. This is how even small, consistent contributions can turn into significant wealth, directly challenging the "not enough money to invest" belief.

Basic Investment Vehicles: Where Your Money Can Go to Work

Forget the complicated trading floors for a moment. Most everyday investors build wealth through a few fundamental vehicles:

1. **Stocks:** When you buy a stock, you're buying a tiny ownership slice of a company. As the company grows and becomes more profitable, the value of your stock can increase, and you might receive a portion of the profits (dividends).
    - *Simple Analogy:* Owning a tiny piece of your favorite coffee shop. If the coffee shop does well, your piece becomes more valuable.
    - *Risk:* Can be volatile. A single company's stock can go up or down significantly.

2. **Bonds:** When you buy a bond, you're essentially lending money to a government or a corporation. In return, they promise to pay you back your original money (principal) by a certain date, plus regular interest payments.
    - *Simple Analogy:* Being the bank for a reliable borrower.
    - *Risk:* Generally less risky than stocks, but also offer lower returns.

3. **Mutual Funds:** These are professionally managed collections (or "baskets") of stocks, bonds, or other investments. When you buy a share of a mutual fund, you're buying a piece of that entire basket.
    - *Simple Analogy:* Instead of buying one apple (a stock), you buy a fruit basket with apples, oranges, and bananas (many different stocks/bonds).
    - *Risk:* Diversified, so generally less volatile than individual stocks.

4. **Exchange-Traded Funds (ETFs):** Similar to mutual funds, ETFs are also baskets of investments, but they trade on stock exchanges like individual stocks.
    - *Simple Analogy:* A slightly more flexible fruit basket that you can buy and sell throughout the day.
    - *Risk:* Diversified, often have lower fees than mutual funds.

For the beginner, particularly those starting from scratch, focusing on diversified funds like Mutual Funds and ETFs is generally recommended over individual stocks. Why? Because they offer instant **diversification**, meaning your money is spread across many different companies or assets, significantly reducing your risk if one particular company struggles. This is crucial for new investors who feel they "don't have enough" to take on high individual stock risk.

Risk vs. Reward: Finding Your Comfort Zone

All investing involves some level of risk. The general rule is: **the higher the potential reward, the higher the risk.**

- **Stocks** generally offer higher long-term returns but come with more short-term volatility.
- **Bonds** are generally less risky and offer lower returns.
- **Diversified funds (Mutual Funds, ETFs)** balance this by combining various assets, moderating risk while still aiming for solid returns.

For most long-term wealth building, especially for retirement, a balanced approach with a significant allocation to diversified stock funds is often recommended, as historically, stocks have provided the best returns over decades.

The Magic of Compound Interest: Your Money's Superpower

We briefly touched on compound interest in Chapter 5 with savings, but in investing, it becomes truly magical. Compound interest is the process where your earnings (interest or investment returns) generate their own earnings. It's money making money, which then makes even more money. Albert Einstein allegedly called it the "eighth wonder of the world."

- **Example:** If you invest $100 and earn 10%, you now have $110. Next year, you earn 10% on $110, not just $100. This snowball effect accelerates dramatically over time, especially over decades.
- **Why this matters for** *you:* This is how even consistent, small contributions from your paycheck-to-paycheck life can grow into significant wealth. You don't need a massive starting sum. You need **consistency and time**. Every dollar you invest today has decades to compound, proving that you *do* have the capacity to build wealth.

Overcoming the Intimidation: How to Get Started

The biggest hurdle is often just taking the first step. Here's how to begin, even if you feel you don't earn enough to be an "investor":

1. **Open an Investment Account:**
   - **Employer-Sponsored Retirement Accounts (e.g., 401(k), 403(b)):** If your

employer offers one, this is often the best place to start.

- **MATCHING FUNDS!** This is free money. If your employer offers to match your contributions (e.g., they contribute $0.50 for every $1 you contribute up to a certain percentage of your salary), contribute at least enough to get the full match. This is an immediate, guaranteed return on your money that you literally cannot get anywhere else. This alone can negate the "not enough" belief.
- **Automatic Deductions:** Contributions come directly from your paycheck, so you don't even see the money, making it easy to stick to.

  - **Individual Retirement Accounts (IRAs):** If you don't have an employer plan, or want to save more, open an IRA (Traditional or Roth).
    - **Roth IRA:** You contribute after-tax money, and your withdrawals in retirement are tax-free. Excellent for those who expect to be in a higher tax bracket in retirement.
    - **Traditional IRA:** Contributions might be tax-deductible now, but withdrawals in retirement are taxed.

  - **Taxable Brokerage Account:** For savings beyond retirement accounts. These accounts don't have the same tax advantages but offer more flexibility.

2. **Start Small:** Many investment platforms and mutual funds allow you to start with as little as $50 or $100. Some even offer "fractional shares," meaning you can buy a tiny piece of a high-priced stock. The important thing is to *start*.
3. **Invest Consistently:** This is the most powerful strategy. Set up automatic monthly transfers from your checking account to your investment account. This is called **dollar-cost averaging**, and it's a brilliant way to smooth out market volatility, ensuring you buy more shares when prices are low and fewer when prices are high. This systematic approach is perfectly suited for an employee on a regular paycheck.
4. **Keep it Simple:** For most beginners, focusing on broad-market index funds or diversified ETFs is ideal. These funds aim to mirror the performance of an entire market (like the S&P 500) and require very little active management. You don't need to pick individual stocks to build wealth.

Actionable Step: Your First Investment Research & Action

1. **Check Your Employer Plan:** If you have one, find out if your employer offers a 401(k)

or similar plan.

- ○ **Crucial Question:** Do they offer an employer match? If yes, how much?
- ○ **Action:** If they do, make it your immediate goal to contribute *at least* enough to get the full match. This is free money for your future!

2. **Explore Investment Account Options:** If you don't have an employer plan, or want to contribute more, research opening a Roth IRA with a reputable brokerage firm (e.g., Fidelity, Vanguard, Charles Schwab). Look for those with low minimums and simple index fund options.

3. **Choose a "Set It and Forget It" Approach:** Decide on an initial amount you can consistently contribute monthly (even $50 or $100 is a fantastic start), drawing from the money freed up in previous chapters. Remember, consistency beats amount initially.

Investing Jargon Buster (Key Terms)

- **Portfolio:** The collection of all your investments.
- **Diversification:** Spreading your investments across different assets to reduce risk.
- **Returns:** The profit or loss generated by your investments.
- **Volatility:** How much an investment's value goes up and down.
- **Index Fund:** A type of mutual fund or ETF that holds a specific group of stocks or bonds to match a market index (e.g., S&P 500).
- **Expense Ratio:** The annual fee charged by a fund, expressed as a percentage of your investment. Lower is better!

Investing is not about getting rich overnight. It's about consistently planting seeds for your financial future. It's about understanding that even from a modest paycheck, when you make your money work through the power of compounding, you are actively building the financial freedom and generational wealth you once thought was out of reach. You *do* earn enough to invest. You just needed the blueprint.

Your Next Steps: Ignite Your Wealth Engine

1. **Investigate Employer Match:** Find out if your employer offers a retirement plan match and how much it is. Prioritize meeting that match.
2. **Choose Your First Investment Vehicle:** Decide between an employer-sponsored plan (if matched), a Roth IRA, or a basic brokerage account.
3. **Set Your Initial Investment Amount:** How much can you realistically automate each month towards investing, starting now? Even $50-$100 is powerful.
4. **Open the Account & Automate the Transfer:** Take the plunge. Open the account and set up that automatic monthly contribution. This is the single most important action you can take in this chapter.

Chapter 7: Retirement Ready: Securing Your Golden Years

You've built incredible momentum. You've bravely confronted your money mindset, mapped out your income and expenses, started demolishing debt, and are now building your financial fortress with an emergency fund. You're consistently saving and investing for various goals. But what about the *long* game? What about ensuring you can enjoy the fruits of your labor in your golden years, without the stress of financial worry?

For many, retirement feels like a distant fantasy, a luxury reserved for those who "have enough" *now*. You might think, "I'm just trying to get by today; I can't possibly think about retirement decades away." Or, "I don't earn enough to save for retirement; I'll just work forever."

These are understandable feelings, but they are also dangerous myths. Retirement planning isn't a privilege; it's a necessity. It's about securing your future independence and freedom. And the truth is, thanks to the magic of compounding, even modest, consistent contributions, started *today*, can build a substantial nest egg for your future, proving you *do* earn enough to secure your golden years.

The Retirement Mirage: Why It Feels Unreachable (and why it isn't)

The idea of saving for retirement can feel overwhelming. It seems so far off, and the numbers can seem astronomical. But the reality is that retirement planning is simply long-term investing with specific tax advantages. It's not about becoming rich quickly; it's about a consistent, disciplined approach over many years.

The cost of *not* planning for retirement is far greater than any perceived sacrifice today. It means:

- Potentially working far longer than you want to.
- Experiencing financial stress and anxiety in your older years.
- Becoming dependent on others for support.
- Missing out on the freedom to pursue your passions in retirement.

The Power of Time & Compounding (Revisited for Retirement)

We touched on the magic of compound interest in earlier chapters, but in the context of retirement, it becomes truly awe-inspiring. Time is your greatest asset. The longer your money has to grow, the more powerful the compounding effect becomes.

Consider this:

- If you consistently save just $100 per month from age 25 to 65, earning an average 8% annual return (achievable with diversified stock investments), you could accumulate over **$340,000**.
- If you delay starting until age 35, saving the same $100 per month, you would only have around **$140,000** by age 65.

The difference is staggering. Time is the key ingredient. This dramatically illustrates how someone who feels they "don't earn enough" *can* become a retirement millionaire. It's not about hitting a financial home run; it's about consistent base hits over decades.

Demystifying Retirement Accounts

The world of retirement accounts can seem complex, but the basic options are straightforward:

- **401(k) / 403(b) (Employer-Sponsored Plans):** If your employer offers one of these plans, it's often the best place to start.
  - **The Employer Match is Free Money:** If your employer matches your contributions (e.g., they contribute $0.50 for every $1 you contribute), contribute *at least* enough to get the full match. This is a guaranteed return on your money that you can't get anywhere else. This alone can negate the "not enough" belief.
  - **Automatic Contributions:** Money is deducted directly from your paycheck, making it easy to save consistently.
  - **Pre-Tax vs. Roth:** You may have a choice between pre-tax contributions (which lower your current taxable income) or Roth contributions (where you pay taxes now, but withdrawals in retirement are tax-free).
  - **Vesting:** Be aware of any vesting schedule (how long you need to work for the company to fully own their contributions).

- **Traditional IRA:** An Individual Retirement Account you can open on your own.
  - Contributions may be tax-deductible, lowering your current taxable income.
  - Your money grows tax deferred.
  - Withdrawals in retirement are taxed as ordinary income.

- **Roth IRA:** Another type of IRA.
  - Contributions are made *after* you've paid taxes on the money.
  - Your money grows tax-free.
  - Qualified withdrawals in retirement are completely *tax-free*.
  - Generally preferred for those who expect to be in a higher tax bracket in retirement, or whose current income means their tax deduction from a Traditional IRA might be minimal. For many starting out, Roth is ideal due to tax-free growth.

- **Solo 401(k) / SEP IRA:** Options for self-employed individuals or those with significant side hustle income.

How Much to Contribute (The "Rule of Thumb" & Personalized Goals)

A common guideline is to aim to save 10-15% of your income for retirement. If that number feels daunting, don't panic. Start small, focusing first on getting any employer match. Then, commit to increasing your contributions by just 1% of your salary each year. Even small increases have a massive impact over time.

Remember, the money you've freed up from demolishing debt (Chapter 3) and the money you've identified through smart budgeting (Chapter 2) can be directly channeled into your retirement savings.

Investing within Retirement Accounts (Again, Keep It Simple)

Opening the retirement account is the first step, but you must also choose how to invest the money *within* the account. For most beginners, particularly in retirement accounts, simplicity is key:

- **Target-Date Funds:** These are the simplest option. You choose a fund based on your approximate retirement year (e.g., a "2050 Target Date Fund"). The fund automatically adjusts its asset allocation (mix of stocks and bonds) over time, becoming more conservative as you approach retirement.
- **Broad-Market Index Funds/ETFs:** As discussed in Chapter 6, these funds aim to mirror the performance of an entire market (like the S&P 500) and require very little active management. They offer instant diversification and are a solid choice for long-term growth.

Avoid the temptation to pick individual stocks within your retirement accounts. Focus on broad diversification for long-term stability.

Catch-Up Contributions & Social Security (Briefly)

If you're age 50 or older, you can make "catch-up" contributions to your retirement accounts, allowing you to save even more. Also, remember that Social Security is designed to be a *supplement* to your retirement income, not your sole source.

The Peace of Mind of a Secure Future

Consistently contributing to your retirement, even if it feels small today, is a profound act of self-care. It's about breaking the cycle of living paycheck-to-paycheck not just today, but for your entire life. It's about securing your independence, your freedom, and your ability to enjoy your golden years with dignity and peace of mind. You *do* earn enough to build this future. You just need to start, and let the magic of compounding work its wonders.

Your Next Steps: Secure Your Tomorrow

1. **Retirement Account Checklist:** Do you have an employer-sponsored retirement plan (401(k) or 403(b))? Are you contributing enough to get the full employer match? If not, make this your top priority.
2. **Roth IRA Exploration:** If you don't have an employer plan, or want to save more, research opening a Roth IRA with a reputable brokerage firm (e.g., Fidelity, Vanguard, Charles Schwab).
3. **Contribution Increase Challenge:** Commit to increasing your retirement contributions by at least 1% of your salary each year. If you don't have a percentage option, set a target dollar amount to increase your contributions by annually.
4. **Retirement Calculator Test:** Use a simple online retirement calculator (many are free) to see the long-term impact of consistent contributions. This can be a powerful motivator.

Chapter 8: Real Estate Riches: Leveraging Property for Wealth

You've built incredible momentum. Your mindset is tuned for abundance, your finances are clear, debt is shrinking, an emergency fund stands guard, and you're consistently saving and investing for retirement and other goals. You might be feeling a sense of control you haven't experienced before. Now, let's explore another powerful avenue for wealth creation that often feels out of reach: **real estate.**

For many, owning a home, let alone an investment property, seems like an impossible dream when you're caught in the paycheck-to-paycheck cycle. The thought of a down payment, mortgages, or managing tenants can feel overwhelming, leading to the familiar whisper, "I don't earn enough to even *think* about real estate."

But here's the truth: real estate, from your first home to strategic investment properties, offers unique and powerful ways to build equity, generate income, and create lasting wealth. It's a tangible asset that can provide both financial security and generational opportunity, proving that significant, tangible assets are within your grasp with careful planning and consistency.

More Than Just a Home: Real Estate as an Asset

Think of your home not just as a place to live, but as an asset actively building wealth for you. When you buy a house, you're not just paying rent; you're engaging in a form of **forced savings**. A portion of every mortgage payment goes towards paying down the **principal** (the actual amount you borrowed), building your **equity** (your ownership stake) over time.

Additionally, while not guaranteed, real estate values generally tend to **appreciate** over the long term. This means your property could be worth more years down the line than what you paid for it. This isn't about getting rich quick, but about understanding how a primary residence can be your first, powerful step into real estate wealth, offering diversification away from just the stock market.

The key, especially when you're building your financial foundation, is to buy a home you can truly **afford.** Don't just look at what the bank *pre-approves* you for; look at what your **budget** (from Chapter 2) tells you you can comfortably manage without sacrificing your other financial goals. Saving for that down payment, as outlined in Chapter 5, is often the biggest hurdle, but it's entirely achievable with discipline.

Beyond Your Home: Investing in Real Estate

Once you've established a solid foundation, you can explore other ways to leverage real estate to build wealth:

- **Rental Properties:** This is where you purchase a property (like a single-family home, duplex, or apartment) and rent it out to tenants.
  - **Income Generation:** The rent you collect can create **positive cash flow** after covering your mortgage, taxes, insurance, and expenses. This provides a direct, consistent income stream.
  - **Appreciation:** Like a primary residence, the property itself can increase in value over time.
  - **Leverage:** You use a bank's money (the mortgage) to control a much larger asset, amplifying your potential returns.
  - **Challenges:** It's not truly "passive" income, especially at first. It requires managing tenants, handling repairs, dealing with vacancies, and budgeting for unexpected capital expenditures (like a new roof or HVAC system). It's a business, and it takes time and effort.

- **Real Estate Investment Trusts (REITs):** If the idea of being a landlord doesn't appeal to you, or you don't have the capital for a direct property purchase, REITs are a fantastic alternative.
  - **What they are:** REITs are companies that own, operate, or finance income-producing real estate across various sectors (apartments, shopping malls, offices, hotels, warehouses).
  - **How they work:** You buy shares in a REIT just like you would a stock. This allows you to invest in a portfolio of real estate without actually owning or managing properties.
  - **Pros:** They offer diversification (as they hold many properties), liquidity (you can buy and sell shares easily), and often pay high dividends because they're legally required to distribute most of their taxable income to shareholders.
  - **Cons:** Their value can fluctuate with the stock market and interest rates.

- **Real Estate Crowdfunding:** This is a newer option where multiple investors pool their money to fund larger real estate projects. You can invest smaller amounts than direct ownership, but it can come with higher risks and less control. Consider this only after you've thoroughly explored other options.

Getting Started in Real Estate (Even with Limited Income)

The path to real estate wealth can begin even if you feel you're starting with limited funds:

- **Education is Key:** Before you buy anything, educate yourself. Learn about your local real estate market, different property types, and landlord-tenant laws if you're considering rentals. Real estate investing is a marathon, not a sprint.
- **Down Payment Savings:** This is often the biggest hurdle. Revisit Chapter 5 and specifically dedicate a portion of your goal-oriented savings to a down payment. Remember those "money leaks" and income expansion ideas from Chapter 9; they are your fuel for this significant goal.
- **"House Hacking":** This is a powerful strategy for employees wanting to get into real estate. You buy a multi-unit property (like a duplex, triplex, or even a house with a basement apartment) and live in one unit while renting out the others to cover the mortgage. The rent from your tenants can significantly offset, or even fully cover, your mortgage payment, allowing you to live for free or very cheaply while building equity and learning about property management.
- **Start Small with REITs:** If direct ownership feels too far off, start by investing in REIT ETFs or mutual funds through your existing investment account (Chapter 6). This gives you exposure to the real estate market, often with a low minimum investment, and helps you understand how property values can contribute to your portfolio.

Risks to Be Aware Of

While real estate is a powerful wealth builder, it's not without its risks:

- **Illiquidity:** Real estate can be harder and slower to sell quickly compared to stocks or funds.
- **Market Fluctuations:** Property values can go down, especially in recessions or local economic downturns.
- **Maintenance & Repair Costs:** Unexpected expenses like a leaky roof or broken furnace can be substantial. Always budget for these.
- **Tenant Issues (for rentals):** Vacancies, property damage, and dealing with difficult tenants are realities of being a landlord.

Real estate empowers you to build tangible wealth, create additional income streams, and ultimately solidify your financial independence. It's a testament to the fact that you *can* expand your financial horizons beyond just a paycheck, and it's a vital component of creating a truly diversified and lasting legacy.

Your Next Steps: Explore Your Property Power

1. **Homeownership Dream Check:** If buying a primary residence is a goal, research average home prices and required down payments in an area you'd like to live. What would your target savings amount be?
2. **REIT Exploration:** Look up a few popular REIT ETFs (e.g., VNQ, IYR) and read their descriptions. Consider allocating a small portion of your investment contributions (from Chapter 6) to a diversified REIT fund to get started.
3. **"House Hacking" Idea Brainstorm:** If this strategy interests you, do some initial research on multi-unit properties in your local area. Could this be a path for you?
4. **Property Investment Learning Plan:** List 2-3 specific resources (books, podcasts, local investor groups, online courses) you will use to learn more about real estate investing in the coming months.

Chapter 9: Income Expansion: Earning More to Invest More

You've learned to manage your money like a pro. You've gotten clear on your budget, you're systematically paying down debt, building your emergency fund, and consistently investing for retirement and other goals. You're doing everything right to maximize every dollar you currently earn.

But for many, especially employees, there's a stubborn belief that your income is a fixed pie, predetermined by your job title or industry. You might think, "I'm already doing everything I can with my current salary. There's no more money to find." This "income ceiling" myth is one of the most limiting beliefs, and it's a direct amplifier of the feeling that you "don't earn enough."

While budgeting helps you optimize your *current* income, true acceleration towards generational wealth often comes from **expanding the pie itself**. This chapter is about unlocking your full earning potential, shattering that "not enough" ceiling, and proving that you *can* generate more income to fuel your financial goals.

Leveraging Your Primary Job

Your current job is likely your most significant income stream, and there's often hidden potential right where you are.

1. **Master the Art of Salary Negotiation:**
    - **Why it matters:** Even a small raise, compounded over years, can add up to hundreds of thousands of dollars in lifetime earnings. Don't leave money on the table.
    - **Research your value:** Use sites like Glassdoor, LinkedIn, and Payscale to understand the market rate for your role, skills, and experience in your geographic area.
    - **Quantify your achievements:** When asking for a raise or promotion, don't just say you're a "hard worker." Detail how you've saved the company money, increased revenue, improved processes, or led successful projects. Use numbers and specifics whenever possible.
    - **Practice:** Rehearse what you'll say. Be confident, professional, and focus on the value you bring to the company.

2. **Seek Promotions and Skill Development:**
   - **Identify skill gaps:** What skills are needed for the next level in your career path? Can you take internal training, online courses, or pursue certifications to bridge those gaps?
   - **Be a problem-solver:** Look for opportunities to take on new responsibilities, lead projects, or solve challenges that get noticed by management.
   - **Network:** Build relationships with colleagues and leaders both inside and outside your department.
   - **Utilize performance reviews:** See these not just as evaluations, but as opportunities to discuss your career trajectory and express your interest in growth and higher compensation.

Side Hustles: Your Income Accelerators

A **side hustle** is a flexible way to earn extra money outside your primary job. This isn't just about spare change; it's about building an additional income stream that can dramatically accelerate your financial progress.

- **Benefits:** Extra side hustle income can be specifically designated to:
  - Pay off debt even faster (Chapter 3).
  - Supercharge your savings goals (Chapter 5) for a down payment or other aspirations.
  - Boost your retirement contributions (Chapter 7) or fuel your investment portfolio (Chapter 6).
  - Test out entrepreneurial ideas with minimal risk.
  - Develop new skills that could lead to a career change or even a full-time business.
- **Brainstorming Ideas (Tap into your skills and interests!):**
  - **Service-Based:** Freelance writing, graphic design, virtual assistant, social media management, web design, dog walking, babysitting, tutoring, handyman services, cleaning.
  - **Gig Economy:** Driving for Uber/Lyft, delivering for DoorDash/Uber Eats, performing tasks on TaskRabbit, online survey sites.
  - **Selling:** Selling unused items online (eBay, Facebook Marketplace), reselling thrift store finds, creating and selling crafts (Etsy), starting a small e-commerce store.
  - **Skill-Based:** Teaching music lessons, offering photography services, providing fitness coaching, coding.

Passive Income Streams: The Ultimate Goal

While "passive" often implies zero effort, it usually means money earned with minimal *ongoing* effort after an initial setup. It's the ideal for true financial freedom.

- **Examples:**
  - **Rental income:** As discussed in Chapter 8, from properties you own.
  - **Dividends:** From your investments (Chapter 6).
  - **Royalties:** From a book, music, or other creative work.
  - **Creating digital products:** Online courses, e-books, templates, stock photos.
  - **Affiliate marketing:** Promoting products and earning a commission.

These streams often require upfront work or capital, but they build wealth that continues to flow even when you're not actively working, creating true financial resilience.

Entrepreneurship: The Long Game

For some, income expansion eventually evolves into full-blown entrepreneurship. Starting your own business is the ultimate way to control your income ceiling, but it requires significant effort, risk, and dedication. Often, it starts as a side hustle that gains traction.

Time Management & Energy Management

You might be thinking, "Where will I find the time?" Earning more often requires an initial investment of time and energy.

- **Prioritize ruthlessly:** What's truly important for your goals?
- **Time audit:** Track how you spend your hours for a week. You might be surprised where you can reclaim time (e.g., less screen time, more intentional planning).
- **Protect your energy:** Don't burn out. Ensure you're still prioritizing self-care, sleep, and relationships. This is a marathon, not a sprint.

The Compounding Effect of Income Growth

Every extra dollar you earn isn't just a single dollar; it's a dollar that can be strategically saved, invested, and compounded over time. This exponentially accelerates your wealth-building journey. This is the ultimate rebuttal to the "not enough" belief. You are now actively creating "more than enough" for yourself and your future, solidifying your path to generational wealth.

Your Next Steps: Unleash Your Earning Power

1. **Salary Negotiation Prep:** If applicable, research the salary range for your role and industry. List 3-5 specific achievements you can quantify and highlight in a raise discussion.
2. **Side Hustle Brainstorm:** Based on your skills, interests, and available time, list 3-5 potential side hustle ideas you could realistically pursue, including initial steps.
3. **Time Audit:** For the next few days, simply track how you spend your time. Look for any hours you could realistically free up for income-generating activities.
4. **Income Expansion Goal:** Set a specific, measurable target for how much extra income you want to generate monthly within the next 3-6 months. Write it down.

Chapter 10: Smart Tax Strategies: Keeping More of Your Money

You've worked tirelessly to earn your income, manage your spending, pay down debt, build savings, invest for your future, and even explore ways to expand your income. You're doing everything right to build wealth. But there's a significant portion of your hard-earned money that disappears before it even hits your bank account, or that you pay out annually: **taxes.**

For many, taxes feel like an unavoidable, complex burden—just another expense that reinforces the feeling of "not enough." You might think, "I already pay so much in taxes, there's nothing I can do about it." This belief is common, but it's also a missed opportunity.

The truth is, taxes are often your largest single expense. By understanding basic tax principles and strategically utilizing tax-advantaged accounts and available deductions, you can legally keep more of your income. Every dollar you save in taxes is a dollar you get to keep and direct towards your financial freedom, your investments, or your generational wealth goals. It's a powerful form of "earning more" without actually getting a raise.

The Hidden Expense: Understanding Taxes

You see your gross salary, and then you see your net pay—the amount that actually lands in your account. The difference? A big chunk of it is taxes: federal income tax, state income tax (if applicable), Social Security, and Medicare.

- **Gross vs. Net Income:** As we discussed in Chapter 2, your net income is what you actually take home. Understanding the deductions from your gross pay is the first step to identifying potential tax savings.
- **Tax Brackets:** Our tax system is progressive. This means different portions of your income are taxed at different rates. For example, the first segment of your income might be taxed at 10%, the next at 12%, and so on. Understanding this helps you see how deductions can lower the amount of your income that falls into higher brackets.
- **Tax Deductions vs. Tax Credits:** This is a crucial distinction:
  - **Tax Deduction:** Reduces your *taxable income*. If you have $50,000 in taxable income and a $1,000 deduction, your taxable income becomes $49,000. This saves you money based on your highest marginal tax bracket.

- **Tax Credit:** Directly reduces your *tax bill dollar-for-dollar.* A $1,000 tax credit means you owe $1,000 less in taxes. Tax credits are generally more powerful than deductions.

Leveraging Tax-Advantaged Accounts (Revisiting & Reinforcing)

Some of the most powerful tax strategies involve using specific accounts designed by the government to encourage saving and investing. We've already touched on these, but let's emphasize their tax benefits:

- **Retirement Accounts (401(k), Traditional IRA):**
  - **Pre-tax contributions:** Money you contribute to these accounts is typically deducted from your taxable income in the year you contribute. This means you pay less in taxes *now*, directly increasing your take-home pay or freeing up more money for other goals. Your investments grow tax-deferred until retirement.
  - **Roth Accounts (Roth IRA, Roth 401(k)):**
    - You contribute *after-tax* money. The magic here is that your money grows completely tax-free, and qualified withdrawals in retirement are also *tax-free.* This is incredibly powerful, especially if you expect to be in a higher tax bracket in retirement.

- **Health Savings Accounts (HSAs):** Often called the "triple tax advantage" account, HSAs are a powerhouse for those with a high-deductible health plan (HDHP).
  - **Tax-deductible contributions:** Lower your taxable income.
  - **Tax-free growth:** Your investments within the HSA grow without being taxed.
  - **Tax-free withdrawals:** When used for qualified medical expenses, withdrawals are tax-free.
  - *Bonus:* After age 65, you can withdraw funds for any purpose, and they'll be taxed as ordinary income, similar to a Traditional IRA. This makes them a stealth retirement account for healthcare costs.

- **529 Plans (for Education Savings):** Briefly mention for those saving for children's education. Contributions to these plans often offer state income tax deductions, and the money grows tax-free when used for qualified education expenses.

Common Deductions & Credits for Employees

While most people take the **standard deduction** (a fixed amount that reduces your taxable income), it's good to be aware of other deductions and credits that might apply to you, especially if your situation changes or if you have a side hustle.

- **Standard Deduction vs. Itemized Deductions:** Explain that most people take the standard deduction now.
- **Student Loan Interest Deduction:** If applicable.
- **Educator Expenses:** If they are a teacher.
- **Child Tax Credit:** If applicable.
- **Earned Income Tax Credit (EITC):** For lower to moderate-income individuals/families (crucial for this audience).
- **Saver's Credit (Retirement Savings Contributions Credit):** For low/moderate-income individuals contributing to retirement accounts (powerful!).
- **Homeowner Deductions:** Mortgage interest, property taxes (if they itemize).

Smart Tax Moves Throughout the Year

Tax planning isn't just an annual event; it's a continuous process:

- **Adjust Your W-4:** This form tells your employer how much tax to withhold from each paycheck. If you consistently get a large refund, you're giving the government an interest-free loan. Adjusting your W-4 can put more money in your pocket throughout the year, which you can then save or invest. Conversely, if you owe a lot, you might need to increase withholding.
- **Keep Meticulous Records:** Especially for side hustles or any potential deductions. Track all income and expenses.
- **Understanding Capital Gains (Briefly):** When you sell an investment for a profit, it's called a capital gain. Long-term capital gains (investments held for over a year) are taxed at lower rates than short-term gains (held for a year or less). This is another reason to invest for the long term.

When to Seek Professional Tax Advice

While understanding the basics is empowering, tax laws can be complex and change frequently. For most employees with straightforward finances, tax software (like TurboTax or H&R Block) can suffice. However, for more complex situations, a qualified tax professional (a Certified Public Accountant - CPA, or an Enrolled Agent - EA) is invaluable.

- **When to consider a professional:**
  - You start a business or have significant side hustle income.
  - You experience major life changes (marriage, divorce, birth of a child, home purchase).
  - You have significant investments or rental properties.
  - You're unsure about specific deductions or credits.
  - You want to optimize your tax strategy for long-term wealth.

A good tax professional can save you far more money than their fee by identifying deductions and strategies you might miss.

The Power of Tax Efficiency

Every dollar you save on taxes is a dollar that can be immediately deployed for your financial goals. It's a direct increase in your financial capacity. This isn't about avoiding taxes illegally; it's about smart, legal planning that allows your money to work harder for *you* rather than being unnecessarily siphoned away. By becoming tax-aware, you are actively taking control of another major expense, reinforcing that you *do* have the capacity to build substantial wealth.

Your Next Steps: Optimize Your Tax Savings

1. **Tax-Advantaged Account Check:** Review your current situation. Are you contributing to your 401(k) (especially if there's a match)? Have you explored opening a Roth IRA? If you have an HDHP, are you utilizing an HSA?
2. **W-4 Review:** Access your W-4 form (usually through your HR department or payroll portal). Consider if you need to adjust your withholding to get more money in your paychecks throughout the year, rather than a large refund at tax time.
3. **Deduction/Credit Scan:** Briefly review the list of common deductions and credits. Do any apply to your situation that you might be missing? Make a note to research them further or ask a tax professional.
4. **Side Hustle Tax Prep (if applicable):** If you have a side hustle, ensure you're meticulously tracking all income and business expenses. This is crucial for tax time.

Part 3: The Legacy - Creating Generational Wealth

Chapter 11: The Power of Giving: Philanthropy & Impact Investing

You've embarked on an incredible financial transformation. You've harnessed your income, conquered debt, built a fortress of security, and set your money on a path to growth. You're building tangible wealth, piece by piece. Now, let's talk about another crucial dimension of true wealth, one that extends beyond your personal balance sheet: the **power of giving.**

For many people navigating the paycheck-to-paycheck struggle, the idea of giving back feels like a luxury reserved only for the ultra-rich. You might think, "I barely have enough for myself; how can I possibly think about giving to others?" This belief that you "don't have enough to give" is understandable, but it's a mindset that limits your perception of abundance.

The truth is, **true generational wealth isn't just about what you accumulate; it's also about the positive impact you create and the values you pass on.** Generosity is a mindset, not just a dollar amount. It can begin even when you're in the building phase, and it's a powerful way to reinforce your own abundance and connect with a purpose larger than yourself.

Why Giving Back Matters

Giving back isn't just about charity; it's about enriching your own life and the lives of those around you.

- **Personal Fulfillment:** Contributing to a cause you care about brings immense joy and satisfaction. It connects you to your community and to a sense of purpose.
- **Modeling for Future Generations:** If you have children or plan to, teaching them about generosity and responsible wealth use from an early age instills invaluable values. This is a foundational piece of generational wealth that extends beyond money.
- **Tax Benefits:** While not the primary motivation, charitable donations can offer tax deductions if you itemize.
- **Community Impact:** Your contributions, no matter how small, strengthen the fabric of society, supporting vital services and initiatives.

Ways to Give Back (Beyond Just Cash)

You don't need a massive bank account to be generous. Your time and talents are just as valuable, especially when you're still building your financial foundation.

1. **Time:** This is often the most accessible way to give. Volunteer for causes you care about:
   - Help at a local food bank or shelter.
   - Mentor a young person.
   - Participate in community cleanup drives.
   - Offer your skills to a non-profit (e.g., website design, accounting, social media help).

2. **Talent:** Leverage your unique skills and expertise. Are you good at writing? Offer to help a small charity with their communications. Are you a great organizer? Help coordinate a fundraising event. Your professional skills can make a huge difference.

3. **Treasure (Money):** As your financial capacity grows, so too can your monetary contributions.
   - **Direct Donations:** Donate directly to charities whose mission aligns with your values.
   - **Micro-Donations:** Even small, consistent contributions can add up. Set up a recurring $5 or $10 automatic transfer to a charity every month, just like you would for your savings goals.
   - **Giving Circles:** Pool your resources with friends or family for a greater collective impact.
   - **Donor-Advised Funds (for larger amounts):** Once you have significant assets, a donor-advised fund allows you to contribute money, receive an immediate tax deduction, and then grant the money to charities over time.

Integrating Values: Impact Investing & ESG

Your money can make a difference even when it's invested for growth. This is where **Impact Investing** comes in. Impact investments are made with the intention to generate not only a financial return but also a positive, measurable social and environmental impact.

- **Environmental, Social, Governance (ESG) Investing:** This is a broader approach where you consider environmental (e.g., climate change, pollution), social (e.g., labor practices, diversity), and governance (e.g., executive compensation, board diversity) factors alongside traditional financial metrics when choosing companies or funds to invest in.

- **How it works:** You can invest in companies that are actively working to solve environmental challenges, promote fair labor practices, or maintain ethical governance. Many mutual funds and ETFs now specialize in ESG or impact investing.
- **Connecting to Generational Wealth:** This is how your money can work for both your financial future and the future of the planet or society your children and grandchildren will inherit. It's a powerful way to leave a multi-faceted legacy. The good news? Many impact and ESG funds have shown strong financial performance, proving you don't necessarily have to sacrifice returns for your values.

Smart Giving Strategies

To make giving a sustainable part of your financial life:

- **Budget for Generosity:** Just like any other expense or saving goal, allocate a specific percentage or amount in your budget for giving. Even 1% of your income, consistently given, can make a difference.
- **Research Charities:** Use reputable sites like Charity Navigator or GuideStar to ensure the organizations you support are transparent and use your donations effectively.
- **Teach Your Children:** Involve children in discussions about giving, volunteering, and values. Let them choose a cause to support or participate in a volunteer activity together. This creates a powerful shared experience.

The Abundance Mindset in Action

Giving is a profound act of financial freedom. It reinforces an **abundance mindset**. When you consciously choose to share your resources, whether it's your time, talent, or treasure, you train your brain to recognize that you *do* have enough to share. This further dismantles the "not enough" belief and empowers you to see your true capacity. It's not about how much you give, but the act of giving itself. It closes the loop on your financial transformation, proving that you have not only achieved personal prosperity but are now contributing to the prosperity of others.

Your Next Steps: Cultivate a Legacy of Generosity

1. **Personal Values Check:** Take a moment to reflect. List 1-2 causes, values, or organizations that you care deeply about. What truly moves you?
2. **Giving Budget:** Allocate a small, consistent amount in your budget for charitable giving. Start with what feels comfortable—even $5 or $10 a month is a fantastic start. Set up an automatic transfer if possible.
3. **Impact Investing Exploration:** If you're investing (from Chapter 6 & 7), research a few ESG or impact-focused ETFs or mutual funds. Could you align some of your investments with your values?
4. **Volunteer/Talent Plan:** Brainstorm one way you could give your time or talent to a cause you care about in the next quarter. Perhaps a few hours on a Saturday, or offering a specific skill.

Chapter 12: Estate Planning: Protecting Your Legacy

You've come full circle on this transformative journey. You've moved from financial anxiety to clarity, from debt to freedom, from saving to strategic investing, and from merely earning to actively expanding your income and giving back. You are not just building wealth for yourself; you are building something that can benefit generations.

But what happens to that wealth, that peace of mind, that future opportunity, if something unexpected happens to you? For many, the topic of **estate planning** feels uncomfortable, even morbid. It's often associated with death, or believed to be only for the extremely rich. You might think, "I don't have enough assets for estate planning," or "It's too complicated right now."

This is a dangerous myth. Estate planning is one of the most loving and responsible things you can do for your family, regardless of your current net worth. It's about protecting your loved ones, ensuring your wishes are honored, and making the transfer of your hard-earned wealth as smooth as possible. It's the final, crucial step in securing your **generational legacy**, preventing your assets from being tied up in courts or distributed against your wishes.

Why Estate Planning Is for Everyone (Not Just the Rich)

No matter your financial situation, basic estate planning is essential. Think of it as a clear roadmap for your assets and your wishes, protecting your family from unnecessary stress and complication during a difficult time.

Without a plan:

- **Your assets could go through probate:** This is a costly, time-consuming public legal process where a court decides how your assets are distributed, often taking months or even years.
- **Your loved ones could face disputes:** Without clear instructions, family members might argue over your belongings or medical decisions, adding emotional strain during grief.
- **Minor children could end up with an unchosen guardian:** If you have children under 18, a court would decide who raises them if you haven't named a guardian, potentially placing them with someone you wouldn't have chosen.
- **Your medical wishes might not be followed:** If you become incapacitated, doctors and family might not know your preferences for healthcare.

Estate planning allows you to control these outcomes, ensuring your wealth continues to serve your family and your values.

Essential Estate Planning Documents (Simplified)

While advanced estate planning can involve complex trusts, the core documents every adult needs are straightforward:

1. **Will (Last Will and Testament):** This is the foundational document. In your will, you designate:
   - Who inherits your assets (money, property, belongings).
   - Who will be the **guardian** for any minor children.
   - Who will be your **executor** (the person responsible for carrying out the instructions in your will).
2. **Durable Power of Attorney (DPOA) for Finances:** This document appoints someone you trust (your "agent" or "attorney-in-fact") to manage your financial affairs if you become incapacitated and can't make decisions for yourself. This person can pay bills, access bank accounts, and handle investments on your behalf, preventing a lengthy court process to appoint a conservator.
3. **Healthcare Power of Attorney / Advance Directive (Living Will):** This appoints someone to make medical decisions for you if you're unable to. An **Advance Directive** (often called a "Living Will") outlines your specific wishes regarding medical treatments (like life support) in end-of-life situations. These documents ensure your healthcare preferences are respected.
4. **Beneficiary Designations:** This is critical! For accounts like **retirement accounts (401(k), IRA), life insurance policies, and some bank accounts**, the beneficiary designation form you fill out with the institution *overrides* what's in your will. Make sure these are updated and accurate, always listing a primary and contingent (backup) beneficiary. Keeping these current ensures your money goes directly to your chosen loved ones without going through probate.
5. **Trusts (Optional, but powerful):** A trust is a legal arrangement that allows a third party (a trustee) to hold assets on behalf of a beneficiary or beneficiaries. While more advanced, a common type, a **Revocable Living Trust**, can help you:
   - **Avoid probate:** Assets held in the trust generally bypass the probate process.
   - **Maintain privacy:** Unlike a will, a trust is usually not a public document.
   - **Control asset distribution:** You can set specific conditions for how and when your beneficiaries receive assets (e.g., at certain ages, for specific purposes).
   - This might be something to consider as your wealth grows or if you have complex family situations.

Key Considerations for Your Legacy

- **Guardianship for Minors:** If you have children under 18, naming a guardian in your will is paramount. Discuss this with your chosen guardians beforehand.
- **Distribution of Assets:** Clearly define who gets what. Be as specific as possible to avoid ambiguity.
- **Digital Assets:** How will your online accounts (social media, email, cryptocurrency, digital photos) be managed? You can grant access or specify deletion.
- **Funeral Wishes:** While not legally binding in all places, outlining your preferences can lighten the burden on loved ones during a difficult time.

The Process: Getting Started

The most challenging part of estate planning is often just starting.

1. **Gather Information:** Make a list of all your assets (bank accounts, investment accounts, real estate, vehicles, valuable possessions) and debts. Note down names and contact information for your proposed executor, guardians, and power of attorney agents.
2. **Seek Professional Help:** Strongly recommend consulting an **estate planning attorney**. An attorney ensures your documents are legally sound for your specific state and situation, and can identify potential issues or needs you didn't even know you had. A good estate planning attorney is an investment in your family's future peace of mind.
3. **Review Regularly:** Life changes—marriage, divorce, the birth of children, buying new assets, moving to a new state—all require you to review and potentially update your plan. Aim for a review every 3-5 years, or after any major life event.

The True Meaning of Generational Wealth

You've worked tirelessly to escape paycheck-to-paycheck and build wealth. Estate planning is the capstone. It ensures that the financial stability, opportunities, and peace of mind you've created will continue to benefit your loved ones for generations. It prevents financial chaos after you're gone and provides a clear path for your legacy to endure. This isn't just about accumulating money; it's about protecting it, sharing it, and ensuring it serves your family's future for years to come. It's the ultimate act of providing security and opportunity for your lineage.

Conclusion: Your Continuous Journey to Generational Prosperity

We've reached the end of our guided journey through building financial freedom. What a transformation you've undergone!

- Remember that feeling of anxiety when your paycheck vanished, or the nagging thought that you "didn't earn enough"? Look how far you've come. You've faced your **money mindset**, gaining clarity and shifting limiting beliefs.
- You've taken control of your finances by meticulously **knowing your numbers** and mastering your budget.
- You've bravely confronted and systematically **demolished debt**, freeing up valuable income.
- You've built a robust **financial fortress** with your emergency fund and essential insurance, safeguarding your progress.
- You've embraced the **power of saving for your goals**, proving that intentional saving can fund your aspirations.
- You've stepped into the exciting world of **investing**, making your money work tirelessly for you through the magic of compounding.
- You've explored strategies for **expanding your income**, shattering that income ceiling and increasing your capacity for wealth building.
- You've learned to be **tax-smart**, ensuring more of your hard-earned money stays in your pocket.
- You've understood the **power of giving**, realizing that true wealth includes positive impact and generosity.
- And finally, you've equipped yourself with the knowledge of **estate planning**, ensuring your legacy and loved ones are protected for generations to come.

This book has provided you with a comprehensive blueprint. It's a testament to the fact that you possess the power to transform your financial reality.

Remember these core principles:

- **Your Mindset is Everything:** The belief that you *can* build wealth is the foundation for all action.
- **Consistency Trumps Intensity:** Small, regular actions, repeated over time, build massive results. You don't need huge windfalls; you need disciplined effort.
- **Knowledge is Power:** The more you understand how money works, the more control you gain.
- **Time and Compounding are Your Greatest Allies:** Start now, stay consistent, and

let time work its magic.
- **You Are Capable:** You've proven it to yourself every step of the way.

Financial freedom isn't a destination that you reach and then stop. It's an ongoing journey of learning, adapting, and growing. There will be new challenges, new opportunities, and new lessons. Embrace them with the same proactive, informed approach you've learned here.

The financial decisions you make today will echo for generations. Step into that power. Embrace your prosperity. And continue to live a life of intentional abundance, knowing you've not only escaped the paycheck-to-paycheck trap but are actively building a truly rich and lasting legacy.

Appendix/Resources: Your Tools for Continued Growth

This section provides additional resources to help you continue your journey.

Glossary of Financial Terms

- **401(k) / 403(b):** Employer-sponsored retirement plans that allow you to save and invest for retirement with tax advantages.
- **Advance Directive:** A legal document outlining your wishes for medical care if you're unable to make decisions.
- **APR (Annual Percentage Rate):** The annual rate of interest charged on borrowed money.
- **Beneficiary Designation:** A form that specifies who inherits the funds in accounts like retirement accounts and life insurance, overriding a will.
- **Compound Interest:** The process where your earnings (interest or investment returns) generate their own earnings, leading to exponential growth.
- **Debt Avalanche:** A debt repayment strategy focusing on paying off the debt with the highest interest rate first.
- **Debt Snowball:** A debt repayment strategy focusing on paying off the smallest debt balance first for motivational wins.
- **Diversification:** Spreading your investments across different assets to reduce risk.
- **Durable Power of Attorney (DPOA):** A legal document appointing someone to manage your finances if you become incapacitated.
- **Emergency Fund:** Money set aside in a separate, easily accessible account specifically for unexpected, unavoidable expenses.
- **Employer Match:** Contributions an employer makes to an employee's retirement account, often based on a percentage of the employee's contribution.
- **Equity (Real Estate):** The portion of a property's value that you own outright (property value minus outstanding mortgage).
- **ESG (Environmental, Social, Governance) Investing:** An investment approach that considers a company's environmental, social, and governance practices alongside financial metrics.
- **ETF (Exchange-Traded Fund):** A type of investment fund that holds a basket of assets (like stocks or bonds) and trades on stock exchanges like individual stocks.
- **Executor:** The person named in a will responsible for carrying out its instructions.
- **Gross Income:** Your total earnings before any taxes or deductions.
- **Guardian:** The person legally responsible for caring for minor children if their parents pass away.
- **HSA (Health Savings Account):** A tax-advantaged savings account for healthcare

expenses, available with high-deductible health plans.

- **HYSA (High-Yield Savings Account):** A savings account that offers a higher interest rate than traditional savings accounts.
- Impact Investing: Investments made with the intention to generate positive, measurable social and environmental impact alongside[2] a financial return.
- Index[3] **Fund:** A type of mutual fund or ETF designed to track the performance of a specific market index.
- **IRA (Individual Retirement Account):** A retirement savings plan that allows individuals to save for retirement with tax benefits.
- **Mutual Fund:** A professionally managed collection of stocks, bonds, or other investments.
- **Net Income:** Your take-home pay after all taxes and deductions have been withheld.
- **Passive Income:** Income generated with minimal ongoing effort after initial setup.
- **Probate:** The legal process of validating a will and administering the estate of a deceased person.
- **REIT (Real Estate Investment Trust):** A company that owns, operates, or finances income-producing real estate; you can buy shares in them like stocks.
- **Roth IRA / Roth 401(k):** Retirement accounts where contributions are made after-tax, but qualified withdrawals in retirement are tax-free.
- **Tax Credit:** A dollar-for-dollar reduction in the amount of tax you owe.
- **Tax Deduction:** An amount that reduces your taxable income.
- **Traditional IRA:** A retirement account where contributions may be tax-deductible, and withdrawals are taxed in retirement.
- **Vesting Schedule:** The timeline for when an employee gains full ownership of employer contributions to a retirement plan.
- **Will (Last Will and Testament):** A legal document expressing a person's wishes as to how their property is to be distributed after their death.

Recommended Books & Podcasts for Continued Learning

- **The Total Money Makeover** by Dave Ramsey (for debt elimination and basic budgeting)
- **The Simple Path to Wealth** by J.L. Collins (for simple index fund investing)
- **I Will Teach You To Be Rich** by Ramit Sethi (for automation and conscious spending)
- **The Psychology of Money** by Morgan Housel (for understanding the behavioral side of finance)
- **Rich Dad Poor Dad** by Robert Kiyosaki (for a different perspective on assets and

liabilities, and entrepreneurship)
- **Podcasts:**
  - **The Ramsey Show** (Financial advice, callers sharing their journey)
  - **ChooseFI** (Financial independence concepts)
  - **Afford Anything** (Investing, real estate, financial freedom)
  - **The Clark Howard Podcast** (Consumer and money saving advice)

Recommended Tools & Apps

- **Budgeting:**
  - **Mint:** Free budgeting and expense tracking.
  - **You Need A Budget (YNAB):** Paid, but powerful for intentional budgeting.
  - **Personal Capital:** Free financial dashboard, helps track net worth.
- **Investing:**
  - **Vanguard, Fidelity, Charles Schwab:** Reputable brokerage firms for IRAs, taxable accounts, and low-cost index funds/ETFs.
  - **M1 Finance, Schwab Intelligent Portfolios:** For automated investing.
- **Debt Management:**
  - **Undebt.it:** Free online tool to visualize debt snowball/avalanche.
- **Tax Preparation:**
  - **TurboTax, H&R Block:** Popular software for filing taxes.
- **Charity Research:**
  - **Charity Navigator, GuideStar:** Websites to research charities and their financial efficiency.

About the Author

Radhesh Reddy Gurrala is not just a financial professional; he is a visionary entrepreneur and a dynamic Champs Leader ignited by a singular mission: to empower every individual and family across all 50 states to seize their financial destiny. He believes with unwavering conviction that living paycheck to paycheck is a choice, not a sentence, and that generational wealth is an achievable reality for anyone armed with the right knowledge and opportunity.

Drawing from his extensive background in building and scaling successful businesses from the ground up, Radhesh brings a uniquely practical and results-driven approach to personal finance. He understands the mechanics of growth, the power of strategic action, and the profound impact of a liberated mindset. This isn't theoretical advice; it's a blueprint forged in the fires of entrepreneurial success and honed through dedicated financial mentorship.

Radhesh has personally guided and built a high-performing team of business partners, watching them transcend financial limitations and achieve remarkable independence through his Proven, Predictable, and Profitable System. His passion stems from seeing lives transformed – from anxiety to abundance, from scarcity to freedom.

Through this book, Radhesh channels his expertise and passion to ignite your own journey. He offers more than just strategies; he offers a pathway to a life where your money works for you, where your dreams are funded, and where your legacy extends far beyond your lifetime.

If you are ready to break free, embrace powerful financial education, unlock true entrepreneurial insight, and join a movement of wealth creators, connect with Radhesh Reddy Gurrala today, Your extraordinary financial future awaits!

LinkedIn: https://www.linkedin.com/in/radheshreddygurrala/

Calendar: https://cal.com/radheshreddygurrala

Made in the USA
Middletown, DE
01 June 2025

76309661R00038